LIVE LIFE

DISCOVERING YOUR NEW LIFE
IN CHRIST

JARRETT PETERO

CONTENTS

WELCOME

DEAR FRIEND
Welcome to LIVE LIFE!

Every person is on a quest: to find the true meaning of life. Deep down, every person is asking the same question: does my life have value? Every person is ultimately seeking the same things: fulfillment and satisfaction. But no matter how hard we try or what we try, value, meaning, fulfillment, and satisfaction remain out of reach. It isn't until we come to the realization that it's not what we are missing that will bring fulfillment, rather it's whom we are missing, and that person is Jesus. He only will bring true satisfaction. To truly live life is to have an active and authentic relationship with God. Are you ready to begin living your new life in Christ?

Jesus said, "I have come that they may have life, and that they may have it more abundantly" (John 10:10).

If you are in Christ, the Bible says you are "a new creation; old things have passed away; behold, all things have become new" (2 Corinthians 5:17). It's a simple truth: you're not the same person that you were before you came to Christ. Your new life in Christ requires that you take the next step. The next step is for you to learn how to daily walk with Christ.

I pray this will be a useful resource as you learn how to live your life for the glory of God. In addition, may you discover the joy of daily walking with Jesus and truly experience the fulfillment of living life!

Jarrett Petero

IF ANYONE IS IN CHRIST, HE IS A NEW CREATION; OLD THINGS HAVE PASSED AWAY; BEHOLD, ALL THINGS HAVE BECOME NEW.
2 CORINTHIANS 5:17

LIVE LIFE :::LIVE FRESH

TOPICS COVERED

WHERE DO I GO FROM HERE?

MY NEW LIFE IN CHRIST

PUT OFF THE OLD LIFE — PUT ON THE NEW LIFE

LIVING JUSTIFIED

LIVE LIFE :::
LIVE FRESH

WHERE DO I GO FROM HERE?
WHAT DO I DO NEXT?

There is nothing in this world more exciting than to know you are going to heaven. Your new life in Christ starts now! However, the first questions new believers often ask after receiving Christ are: Where do I go from here? What do I do next? LIVE LIFE is designed to answer these questions and help you get started in your new relationship with Christ.

Let's begin with the A, B, C, and Ds of the Gospel.

When you agree with what God has said about Himself in the Scriptures and agree with what God has said about your sinful condition, it allows you to see your need for a Savior. As you agree, you then are faced with believing and receiving God's solution to your sin problem through His Son. It's by believing in your heart and mind that Jesus willingly sacrificed Himself on the cross in your place. He was then buried, and three days later, was resurrected from the dead. Upon believing, you willingly confess with your mouth and your life that Jesus is Lord. For it is within your heart that you believe and with the mouth confession is made unto salvation. Now that you have agreed, believed, and confessed, you are called by God to be a doer of the Word of God. Being a doer of the Word of God means you take up your cross and follow Jesus. This is your next step and the key to living life. As you can see, it's important to **agree**, **believe**, **confess**, and then **do** or **follow Jesus**. Are you ready to follow Jesus? It is my belief that by the time you receive this booklet, you have already taken the first step in your new commitment to Christ.

Notice the letter "A" stands for **Agree**. The letter "B" is for **Believe**. The letter "C" is for **Confess**, and "D" for **Do** (to follow Christ is to become His disciple). You have agreed and accepted Christ as your personal Savior. You have believed and confessed that Jesus is your Lord and Savior, and now, it is your desire to follow Him.

A. AGREE
The Gospel is for anyone and everyone who believes. Do you **agree**?

FOR I AM NOT ASHAMED OF THE GOSPEL OF CHRIST, FOR IT IS THE POWER OF GOD TO SALVATION FOR EVERYONE WHO BELIEVES. ROMANS 1:16

The Gospel is for all who have sinned. Do you **agree**?

> THERE IS NONE RIGHTEOUS, NO, NOT ONE; THERE IS NONE WHO UNDERSTANDS; THERE IS NONE WHO SEEKS AFTER GOD. ... FOR ALL HAVE SINNED AND FALL SHORT OF THE GLORY OF GOD.
> ROMANS 3:10-11, 23

The Gospel is for all sinners. Do you **agree**?

> BUT GOD DEMONSTRATES HIS OWN LOVE TOWARD US, IN THAT WHILE WE WERE STILL SINNERS, CHRIST DIED FOR US.
> ROMANS 5:8

B. BELIEVE

To live fresh is to know that you are a new creation.

> THEREFORE, IF ANYONE IS IN CHRIST, HE IS A NEW CREATION; OLD THINGS HAVE PASSED AWAY; BEHOLD, ALL THINGS HAVE BECOME NEW. 2 CORINTHIANS 5:17

> **The moment you called on the name of the Lord to save you, forgive you, and renew your life, you were born anew. This means that you now have a new life. Your new life is based on your personal and daily relationship with Christ. It's all because of the finished work that Jesus accomplished on the cross and His resurrection from the dead that you are now able to truly live life.** To live fresh is to daily discern God's plan and learn to walk with Him daily.

The Gospel is for those who **believe** with their **heart**. Do you **believe**? The Gospel is for those who **believe in Him**. Do you **believe**?

C. CONFESS
The Gospel is for those who **confess** that **Jesus is Lord**. Have you **confessed**?

IF YOU CONFESS WITH YOUR MOUTH THE LORD JESUS AND BELIEVE IN YOUR HEART THAT GOD HAS RAISED HIM FROM THE DEAD, YOU WILL BE SAVED. FOR WITH THE HEART ONE BELIEVES UNTO RIGHTEOUSNESS, AND WITH THE MOUTH CONFESSION IS MADE UNTO SALVATION. FOR "WHOEVER CALLS ON THE NAME OF THE LORD SHALL BE SAVED."
ROMANS 10:9-10, 13

The Gospel is for those **confess** unto **salvation**. Have you **confessed**?

> FOR GOD SO LOVED THE WORLD THAT HE GAVE HIS ONLY BEGOTTEN SON, THAT WHOEVER BELIEVES IN HIM SHOULD NOT PERISH BUT HAVE EVERLASTING LIFE.
> JOHN 3:16

> AND THIS IS ETERNAL LIFE, THAT THEY MAY KNOW YOU, THE ONLY TRUE GOD, AND JESUS CHRIST WHOM YOU HAVE SENT. JOHN 17:3

D. DISCIPLE
The Gospel instructs those on how to be a disciple.

> AND WHOEVER DOES NOT BEAR HIS CROSS AND COME AFTER ME CANNOT BE MY DISCIPLE. LUKE 14:27

The Gospel is for those ready to **forsake** all.

SO LIKEWISE, WHOEVER OF YOU DOES NOT FORSAKE ALL THAT HE HAS CANNOT BE MY DISCIPLE. LUKE 14:33

Then Jesus said to His disciples,

IF ANYONE DESIRES TO COME AFTER ME, LET HIM DENY HIMSELF, AND TAKE UP HIS CROSS, AND FOLLOW ME. MATTHEW 16:24

The Gospel is for those willing to **follow** Christ.

The Gospel is for those who desire to become **true disciples**.

Will you be a disciple and follow Jesus?

BIBLE

The Bible is God's spoken Word. It reveals God's will and work for our lives. The Bible instructs us on how to live life—an abundant life. It equips us to know and to grow. The Bible shows us how to live our life for God.

FOR THE WORD OF GOD IS LIVING AND POWERFUL, AND SHARPER THAN ANY TWO-EDGED SWORD, PIERCING EVEN TO THE DIVISION OF SOUL AND SPIRIT, AND OF JOINTS AND MARROW, AND IS A DISCERNER OF THE THOUGHTS AND INTENTS OF THE HEART. HEBREWS 4:12

ALL SCRIPTURE IS GIVEN BY INSPIRATION OF GOD, AND IS PROFITABLE FOR DOCTRINE, FOR REPROOF, FOR CORRECTION, FOR INSTRUCTION IN RIGHTEOUSNESS, THAT THE MAN OF GOD MAY BE COMPLETE, THOROUGHLY EQUIPPED FOR EVERY GOOD WORK. 2 TIMOTHY 3:16-17

THEREFORE, LAYING ASIDE ALL MALICE, ALL DECEIT, HYPOCRISY, ENVY, AND ALL EVIL SPEAKING, AS NEWBORN BABES, DESIRE THE PURE MILK OF THE WORD, THAT YOU MAY GROW THEREBY, IF INDEED YOU HAVE TASTED THAT THE LORD IS GRACIOUS. 1 PETER 2:1-3

HOW TO READ THE BIBLE

1. Be Intentional. Start with asking God to show you who He is and how He has revealed Himself in the Scriptures. When Jesus was with His disciples, He told them that they would have help in understanding God's will from the Scriptures through the guidance of the Holy Spirit.

HOWEVER, WHEN HE, THE SPIRIT OF TRUTH, HAS COME, HE WILL GUIDE YOU INTO ALL TRUTH; FOR HE WILL NOT SPEAK ON HIS OWN AUTHORITY, BUT WHATEVER HE HEARS HE WILL SPEAK; AND HE WILL TELL YOU THINGS TO COME. JOHN 16:13

Here is a good Bible verse for you to pray that will prepare you to receive instruction from God's Word:

OPEN MY EYES, THAT I MAY SEE WONDROUS THINGS FROM YOUR LAW. PSALM 119:18

2. Be Inquisitive. Ask these six questions. Who, What, When, Where, Why, and How?

- **Who** is writing? And who is the audience?
- **What** is being said and to whom? What did it mean to them?
- **What** is the main principle being taught? What does this reveal about God's character?
- **When** was it written? Historically, what is happening?
- **Where** is it taking place? What type of culture is it?
- **Why** is this important to God? Why should it be important to me?
- **How** does it directly apply to me today?

YOUR WORD I HAVE HIDDEN IN MY HEART, THAT I MIGHT NOT SIN AGAINST YOU.
PSALM 119:11

3. Be Consistent. Set a regular time to read your Bible. It may be ten minutes a day or even twenty minutes a day. Regardless of the amount or quantity of time you spend, it's more important that you spend quality and consistent time reading your Bible. The Bible is where God has revealed His will and work. It's through the Bible that God has primarily chosen to speak to us. Remember, the important thing is that you read it consistently.

SO THEN FAITH COMES BY HEARING, AND HEARING BY THE WORD OF GOD.
ROMANS 10:17

You need to make Bible reading a part of your daily life. It will increase your faith and your spiritual growth. In addition, it will help to keep you from sin and allow you to begin to identify God's will for your life.

For an easy-to-manage, daily reading schedule, Google "**Gospel Coalition two-year Bible reading plan**." This will direct you to a great article about daily reading and has a downloadable schedule for your phone, computer, or tablet.

PRAYER

Prayer is God's invitation for us to directly speak with Him. Prayer is a privilege because it allows us access into God's presence where we can boldly approach His throne of grace and receive mercy when we need it most. Prayer says that we are dependent upon God's wisdom and His strength.

Here are a few Scriptures that remind us of the importance of prayer:

LET US THEREFORE COME BOLDLY TO THE THRONE OF GRACE, THAT WE MAY OBTAIN MERCY AND FIND GRACE TO HELP IN TIME OF NEED. HEBREWS 4:16

NOW THIS IS THE CONFIDENCE THAT WE HAVE IN HIM, THAT IF WE ASK ANYTHING ACCORDING TO HIS WILL, HE HEARS US. AND IF WE KNOW THAT HE HEARS US, WHATEVER WE ASK, WE KNOW THAT WE HAVE THE PETITIONS THAT WE HAVE ASKED OF HIM. 1 JOHN 5:14-15

REJOICE ALWAYS, PRAY WITHOUT CEASING, IN EVERYTHING GIVE THANKS; FOR THIS IS THE WILL OF GOD IN CHRIST JESUS FOR YOU. 1 THESSALONIANS 5:16-18

To live fresh is being able to approach God with confidence, trusting that He is faithful to answer your prayers.

A good way to practice praying is to actually pray through Jesus' prayer model. Notice that our prayer should begin with praise and end with praise. It is by acknowledging how great our Heavenly Father is, which in turn allows us to remember from start to finish just how invested He is in every aspect of our daily lives. Look below and prayerfully read through Jesus' prayer, then make it your own.

OUR FATHER IN HEAVEN,
HALLOWED BE YOUR NAME.
YOUR KINGDOM COME.
YOUR WILL BE DONE
ON EARTH AS IT IS IN HEAVEN.
GIVE US THIS DAY OUR DAILY BREAD.
AND FORGIVE US OUR DEBTS,
AS WE FORGIVE OUR DEBTORS.
AND DO NOT LEAD US INTO TEMPTATION,
BUT DELIVER US FROM THE EVIL ONE.
FOR YOURS IS THE KINGDOM AND THE
POWER AND THE GLORY FOREVER. AMEN.
MATTHEW 6:9-13

PRAY LIKE JESUS

As you review the Lord's prayer, write below which verse or verses correspond to the following words.

- **Praise -** Our Father in heaven, hallowed be Your name. _____

- **Petition -** _____

- **Provision -** _____

- **Pardon -** _____

- **Protection -** _____

- **Praise -** _____

What did you discover and experience as you prayed through Jesus' prayer?

_____

_____

AND WHATEVER YOU ASK IN MY NAME, THAT I WILL DO, THAT THE FATHER MAY BE GLORIFIED IN THE SON. IF YOU ASK ANYTHING IN MY NAME, I WILL DO IT. JOHN 14:13-14

CASTING ALL YOUR CARE UPON HIM, FOR HE CARES FOR YOU. 1 PETER 5:7

BE ANXIOUS FOR NOTHING, BUT IN EVERYTHING BY PRAYER AND SUPPLICATION, WITH THANKSGIVING, LET YOUR REQUESTS BE MADE KNOWN TO GOD; AND THE PEACE OF GOD, WHICH SURPASSES ALL UNDERSTANDING, WILL GUARD YOUR HEARTS AND MINDS THROUGH CHRIST JESUS. PHILIPPIANS 4:6-7

COMMUNITY

When you commit your life to Jesus Christ, you become a part of God's family. The life God intends for you to enjoy is more than just believing; it includes belonging to the community of Christ. This is why it's important for you to be involved and invested in a Christ-centered community group where you can learn, grow, and develop as a believer. Notice what Scripture has to say about the importance of being in fellowship or community in the body of Christ.

> **AND THEY CONTINUED STEADFASTLY IN THE APOSTLES' DOCTRINE AND FELLOWSHIP, IN THE BREAKING OF BREAD, AND IN PRAYERS.** ACTS 2:42

We gather together in community to worship God and be instructed about the things of God.

> **AND LET US CONSIDER ONE ANOTHER IN ORDER TO STIR UP LOVE AND GOOD WORKS, NOT FORSAKING THE ASSEMBLING OF OURSELVES TOGETHER, AS IS THE MANNER OF SOME, BUT EXHORTING ONE ANOTHER, AND SO MUCH THE MORE AS YOU SEE THE DAY APPROACHING.** HEBREWS 10:24-25

We gather together in community to love and encourage one another.

Why is community important to your walk with Christ?

Are you involved or invested in a Christ-centered community? What is the difference?

PUT OFF THE OLD LIFE – PUT ON THE NEW LIFE

Your **new life** is a **fresh life** because God has taken away your old nature, habits, and addictions and has replaced them with a new life. This new nature has transformed your mind to the mind of Christ. For many of us, sin came way too easily, and unfortunately, we enjoyed sin too much. If we were to be categorized, we would be labeled as professional sinners. Why is it that no matter how much we tried to satisfy our flesh with personal pleasure, it always left us disillusioned, empty, and discontented?

The Bible says that sin is pleasurable for a season, but its end always leads to destruction!

So, how do we end this vicious and reckless cycle? The answer is given to us by simply **putting off our old behavior** and replacing it by **putting on our new behavior**.

> **PUT OFF, CONCERNING YOUR FORMER CONDUCT, THE OLD MAN WHICH GROWS CORRUPT ACCORDING TO THE DECEITFUL LUSTS, AND BE RENEWED IN THE SPIRIT OF YOUR MIND, AND THAT YOU PUT ON THE NEW MAN WHICH WAS CREATED ACCORDING TO GOD, IN TRUE RIGHTEOUSNESS AND HOLINESS.**
> EPHESIANS 4:22-24

How do we put off the old nature and put on the new nature?

We put off the old nature in two ways. We commit our old nature to God practically and prayerfully. First, we must commit our actual bodies to God practically. We do this by committing our eyes, ears, hands, and feet to God. Second, we do this by removing ourselves from the places we used to go to participate in sin. We do this by getting rid of the past paraphernalia that would tempt or draw us back into sin. We must look around and throw away anything that causes us to stumble and fall into sin. As we take these practical steps of putting off the old nature and replacing it with the new nature, we pray that God would continue to show us and strengthen us as we walk with Him. As we present our bodies **practically** to God and commit our mind **prayerfully** to God, we will begin to experience God's perfect will for our lives.

I BESEECH YOU THEREFORE, BRETHREN, BY THE MERCIES OF GOD, THAT YOU PRESENT YOUR BODIES A LIVING SACRIFICE, HOLY, ACCEPTABLE TO GOD, WHICH IS YOUR REASONABLE SERVICE. AND DO NOT BE CONFORMED TO THIS WORLD, BUT BE TRANSFORMED BY THE RENEWING OF YOUR MIND, THAT YOU MAY PROVE WHAT IS THAT GOOD AND ACCEPTABLE AND PERFECT WILL OF GOD. ROMANS 12:1-2

LIVING JUSTIFIED

> To be justified means that God has declared us righteous through Jesus Christ. Justification is not a process; it is the instantaneous and unchanging act of God. Justification gives us a new and right standing before God.

To live justified means that your standing with God is **permanent** and **eternal**. Justification is not the same as forgiveness. The difference between forgiveness and justification is that forgiveness can and does occur over and over as we confess our sins to Christ.

> **IF WE CONFESS OUR SINS, HE IS FAITHFUL AND JUST TO FORGIVE US OUR SINS AND TO CLEANSE US FROM ALL UNRIGHTEOUSNESS.** 1 JOHN 1:9

Now, justification happened instantaneously the moment you came to Christ. Justification is a once and for all right standing before God—it's permanent. However, although you are and were forgiven, forgiveness can and will continue each time you confess your sins to Christ. So as you can see, justification and forgiveness go hand in hand.

Justification permanently removes our sin problem once and for all and allows us to have a right standing before God.

To live fresh is to know that God has permanently removed your sin. You are justified.

JUSTIFICATION HAS TWO PARTS, THE CROSS AND THE CROSSOVER

- **The Cross - We are declared not guilty** because our sins were placed upon Christ and paid for by Christ on the cross.

- **The Crossover - We are declared righteous** because all of Christ's righteousness was placed on us.

GOD WAS IN CHRIST RECONCILING THE WORLD TO HIMSELF, NOT IMPUTING THEIR TRESPASSES TO THEM ... FOR HE MADE HIM WHO KNEW NO SIN TO BE SIN FOR US, THAT WE MIGHT BECOME THE RIGHTEOUSNESS OF GOD IN HIM.
2 CORINTHIANS 5:19, 21

FOR WE OURSELVES WERE [PAST TENSE] ALSO ONCE FOOLISH, DISOBEDIENT, DECEIVED, SERVING VARIOUS LUSTS AND PLEASURES, LIVING IN MALICE AND ENVY, HATEFUL AND HATING ONE ANOTHER. BUT WHEN THE KINDNESS AND THE LOVE OF GOD OUR SAVIOR TOWARD MAN APPEARED, NOT BY WORKS OF RIGHTEOUSNESS WHICH WE HAVE DONE, BUT ACCORDING TO HIS MERCY HE SAVED US, THROUGH THE WASHING OF REGENERATION AND RENEWING OF ...

... THE HOLY SPIRIT, WHOM HE POURED OUT ON US ABUNDANTLY THROUGH JESUS CHRIST OUR SAVIOR, THAT HAVING BEEN JUSTIFIED BY HIS GRACE WE SHOULD BECOME HEIRS ACCORDING TO THE HOPE OF ETERNAL LIFE. TITUS 3:3-7

FOR ALL HAVE SINNED AND FALL SHORT OF THE GLORY OF GOD, BEING JUSTIFIED FREELY BY HIS GRACE THROUGH THE REDEMPTION THAT IS IN CHRIST JESUS, WHOM GOD SET FORTH AS A PROPITIATION BY HIS BLOOD, THROUGH FAITH, TO DEMONSTRATE HIS RIGHTEOUSNESS, BECAUSE IN HIS FORBEARANCE GOD HAD PASSED OVER THE SINS THAT WERE PREVIOUSLY COMMITTED, TO DEMONSTRATE AT THE PRESENT TIME HIS RIGHTEOUSNESS, THAT HE MIGHT BE JUST AND THE JUSTIFIER OF THE ONE WHO HAS FAITH IN JESUS. ROMANS 3:23-26

THEREFORE, AS THROUGH ONE MAN'S OFFENSE (ADAM) JUDGMENT CAME TO ALL MEN, RESULTING IN CONDEMNATION, EVEN SO THROUGH ONE MAN'S (JESUS) RIGHTEOUS ACT THE FREE GIFT CAME TO ALL MEN, RESULTING IN JUSTIFICATION OF LIFE. FOR AS BY ONE MAN'S DISOBEDIENCE MANY WERE MADE SINNERS, SO ALSO BY ONE MAN'S OBEDIENCE MANY WILL BE MADE RIGHTEOUS. ROMANS 5:18-19

THEREFORE, HAVING BEEN JUSTIFIED BY FAITH, WE HAVE PEACE WITH GOD THROUGH OUR LORD JESUS CHRIST. ROMANS 5:1

DISCOVER ///
Truth/Scripture Insight/Spirit Insight

Read 2 Corinthians 5:17.

List some old things that have passed away: _____

_____

List some things that have become new: _____

_____

Read 1 Peter 2:1-3 and Romans 10:17.

The Word of God helps us to _____

_____

The Word of God increases our _____

_____

Read Philippians 4:6-9.

What are some of the things we can do to keep ourselves from anxiety?

_____

_____

_____

_____

In learning to "pray like Jesus" (Matthew 6:9-13), how has this helped you to discover the value of prayer?

_____

_____

_____

Community

According to Acts 2:42-47, there are four main essentials that truly characterize the early church. What are these four essentials?

_____

_____

_____

Read Ephesians 4:22-24 and Romans 12:1-2.
How are we to put off the old nature?

_____

_____

How are we to put on the new nature?

_____

_____

Read Titus 3:3-7/Romans 5:18-19
Living justification means:

_____

_____

DECIDE ///
Change of Mind/Believe

How would you describe your new life in Christ?

_____

_____

_____

_____

DO ///
Commit/Take Action
What are two ways that you can take action and experience living a fresh life?

1. _____

2. _____

DEVOTE ///
Invest Time/Continue
Bible reading and prayer time plan

Investing in a Bible is important. All Bibles come in different sizes and shapes. It all depends on what you are looking for in a Bible, like additional study notes, commentary notes, and maps. Here are a few version suggestions: New King James (NKJV), New International (NIV), English Standard (ESV), or New Living Translation (NLT).

As you daily devote yourself to reading your Bible, you will begin to experience spiritual growth and a greater understanding of God's will for your life. We suggest that you read from the New Testament, staring in the book of Luke.

Now, write the best time of day for you to schedule daily Bible reading and prayer:

_____

_____

DEVELOP ///
Experience/Abide

To really help you develop as a believer, it's important that you attend a Christ-centered church and participate in a community group.

What church do you attend?

_____

What community group are you involved in?

_____

When and where does this group meet?

_____

How do you get involved in this group?

_____

MEMORIZE ///

THEREFORE, IF ANYONE IS IN CHRIST, HE IS A NEW CREATION; OLD THINGS HAVE PASSED AWAY; BEHOLD, ALL THINGS HAVE BECOME NEW. 2 CORINTHIANS 5:17

AND YOU SHALL
KNOW THE
TRUTH AND THE
TRUTH SHALL
MAKE YOU FREE
... THEREFORE, IF
THE SON MAKES
YOU FREE, YOU
SHALL BE FREE
INDEED.
JOHN 8:32, 36

LIVE LIFE ::: LIVE FREE

LIVE LIFE :::
LIVE FREE

WHAT DOES IT MEAN TO LIVE FREE?

Sin entangles and strangles us from fully experiencing true freedom. Sin will always bring shame, guilt, and condemnation. Sin has a way of keeping us in a place of psychological despair, discouragement, and doubt. Sin tries to separate us from the sacrificial love of God. Yet, most of all sin steals away our life, and ultimately, sin kills.

To live free begins with knowing that Jesus died on the cross to set us free from the nature of sin, the bondage of sin, and the consequences of sin.

To live free means daily experiencing and expressing the power over past sin, habits, and addictions.

AND YOU HE MADE ALIVE, WHO WERE
DEAD IN TRESPASSES AND SINS, IN ...

37

... WHICH YOU ONCE WALKED ACCORDING TO THE COURSE OF THIS WORLD, ACCORDING TO THE PRINCE OF THE POWER OF THE AIR, THE SPIRIT WHO NOW WORKS IN THE SONS OF DISOBEDIENCE, AMONG WHOM ALSO WE ALL ONCE CONDUCTED OURSELVES IN THE LUSTS OF OUR FLESH, FULFILLING THE DESIRES OF THE FLESH AND OF THE MIND, AND WERE BY NATURE CHILDREN OF WRATH, JUST AS THE OTHERS. BUT GOD, WHO IS RICH IN MERCY, BECAUSE OF HIS GREAT LOVE WITH WHICH HE LOVED US, EVEN WHEN WE WERE DEAD IN TRESPASSES, MADE US ALIVE TOGETHER WITH CHRIST (BY GRACE YOU HAVE BEEN SAVED).
EPHESIANS 2:1-5

HAVING BEEN SET FREE FROM SIN, YOU BECAME SLAVES OF RIGHTEOUSNESS.
ROMANS 6:18

The reality is that before we came to Christ, we were **dead** in sin. We were under the influence and in bondage to sin. We were controlled by our self-centered, sinful nature. However, the moment we turned from our sin and surrendered our life to God, He made us alive together with Christ. Now we are a new creation in Christ.

TEMPTATION

> Temptation is everywhere and comes in many different forms and different colors. No one is immune. Temptation is common to all humanity; however, it's important to know that temptation is not sin. Temptation has one goal—to lead us astray and into sin. Temptation is real, and the struggle is real.

NO TEMPTATION HAS OVERTAKEN YOU EXCEPT SUCH AS IS COMMON TO MAN; BUT GOD IS FAITHFUL, WHO WILL NOT ALLOW YOU TO BE TEMPTED BEYOND WHAT YOU ARE ABLE, BUT WITH THE TEMPTATION WILL ALSO MAKE THE WAY OF ESCAPE, THAT YOU MAY BE ABLE TO BEAR IT. 1 CORINTHIANS 10:13

FOR WE DO NOT HAVE A HIGH PRIEST WHO CANNOT SYMPATHIZE WITH OUR WEAKNESSES, BUT WAS IN ALL POINTS TEMPTED AS WE ARE, YET WITHOUT SIN. HEBREWS 4:15

Jesus was in all points tempted, yet without sin.

READ // LUKE 4:1-3

Notice that Jesus was tempted by the devil for forty days. But when Jesus overcame the temptations the devil initiated, he departed from Jesus until "an opportune time." Satan is always waiting for another chance to tempt us regardless if we are ready or not. When Satan tempts us, we must remain faithful to God and rely on His Word to overcome.

Jesus was tempted but overcame the temptation by using the Word of God.

BE SOBER, BE VIGILANT; BECAUSE YOUR ADVERSARY THE DEVIL WALKS ABOUT LIKE A ROARING LION, SEEKING WHOM HE MAY DEVOUR. 1 PETER 5:8

> **WATCH AND PRAY, LEST YOU ENTER INTO TEMPTATION. THE SPIRIT INDEED IS WILLING, BUT THE FLESH IS WEAK.**
> MATTHEW 26:41

Where do temptations come from?

> **DO NOT LOVE THE WORLD OR THE THINGS IN THE WORLD. IF ANYONE LOVES THE WORLD, THE LOVE OF THE FATHER IS NOT IN HIM. FOR ALL THAT IS IN THE WORLD— THE LUST OF THE FLESH, THE LUST OF THE EYES, AND THE PRIDE OF LIFE—IS NOT OF THE FATHER BUT IS OF THE WORLD. AND THE WORLD IS PASSING AWAY, AND THE LUST OF IT; BUT HE WHO DOES THE WILL OF GOD ABIDES FOREVER.** 1 JOHN 2:15-17

Temptation can come from four areas: the devil, the lust of the flesh, the lust of the eyes, or the pride of life. When temptation arises, it's important for us to **identify** which source or sources that we are being tempted in and use the appropriate Scripture to overcome the temptation. The key to overcoming temptation is to memorize Scripture and use it as a **weapon** against the temptation.

> **BLESSED IS THE MAN WHO ENDURES TEMPTATION; FOR WHEN HE HAS BEEN APPROVED, HE WILL RECEIVE THE CROWN OF LIFE WHICH THE LORD HAS PROMISED TO THOSE WHO LOVE HIM. LET NO ONE SAY WHEN HE IS TEMPTED, "I AM TEMPTED BY GOD"; FOR GOD CANNOT BE TEMPTED BY EVIL, NOR DOES HE HIMSELF TEMPT ANYONE. BUT EACH ONE IS TEMPTED WHEN HE IS DRAWN AWAY BY HIS OWN DESIRES AND ENTICED. THEN, WHEN DESIRE HAS CONCEIVED, IT GIVES BIRTH TO SIN; AND SIN, WHEN IT IS FULL-GROWN, BRINGS FORTH DEATH.**
> JAMES 1:12-15

What happens if a temptation overtakes me?

When we are overcome by a temptation, we must confess it to God, ask for forgiveness, and learn from it; but most importantly, we must turn from it. All sin will ever do is bring death. Recognize that sin is always specific. Sin happens when our lustful desire connects with an enticement or temptation. In the beginning, our desire (like a birth analogy) is conceived, then it grows, being undetected; then it develops and gives birth to sin. However, sin grows, and ultimately, when it is full-grown, brings forth death. Repeated defeat from a temptation is a repeated sin, habit, and addiction. Sin always gives birth to death. To live free is to experience the freedom and forgiveness in Christ from all the shame and guilt of sin.

> **THEREFORE SUBMIT TO GOD. RESIST THE DEVIL AND HE WILL FLEE FROM YOU.**
> JAMES 4:7

> **HE WHO IS IN YOU IS GREATER THAN HE WHO IS IN THE WORLD.**
> 1 JOHN 4:4b

To live free is to experience the freedom and forgiveness in Christ from all of our past shame and guilt.

SPIRITUAL WARFARE
WAR!

You are enlisted as a solider. There are many enlisted, yet so few are engaged in spiritual battle. We are called to fight the good fight of faith because Jesus has already overcome the opposition and won the WAR! Spiritual warfare keeps us in spiritual shape. Yet, we are not called to do it alone; we are to rely upon the power of His might and stand strong in the Lord. The popular saying goes, "never bring a knife to a gun fight." And we should never fight our battles in the flesh but in the Spirit. If we try to fight spiritual battles in the flesh, then we have already lost the fight before it even begins. Too often, we try overcoming the flesh by fleshly weapons. To achieve victory, we must put on the spiritual armor of God and stand against the attacks of the enemy in the power and strength of Christ.

BE STRONG IN THE LORD AND IN THE POWER OF HIS MIGHT. PUT ON THE WHOLE ARMOR OF GOD, THAT YOU MAY BE ABLE TO STAND AGAINST THE WILES OF THE DEVIL. FOR WE DO NOT WRESTLE AGAINST FLESH AND BLOOD, BUT AGAINST PRINCIPALITIES, AGAINST POWERS, AGAINST THE RULERS OF THE DARKNESS OF THIS AGE, AGAINST ...

... SPIRITUAL HOSTS OF WICKEDNESS IN THE HEAVENLY PLACES. THEREFORE, TAKE UP THE WHOLE ARMOR OF GOD, THAT YOU MAY BE ABLE TO WITHSTAND IN THE EVIL DAY, AND HAVING DONE ALL, TO STAND. STAND THEREFORE, HAVING GIRDED YOUR WAIST WITH TRUTH, HAVING PUT ON THE BREASTPLATE OF RIGHTEOUSNESS, AND HAVING SHOD YOUR FEET WITH THE PREPARATION OF THE GOSPEL OF PEACE; ABOVE ALL, TAKING THE SHIELD OF FAITH WITH WHICH YOU WILL BE ABLE TO QUENCH ALL THE FIERY DARTS OF THE WICKED ONE. AND TAKE THE HELMET OF SALVATION, AND THE SWORD OF THE SPIRIT, WHICH IS THE WORD OF GOD; PRAYING ALWAYS WITH ALL PRAYER AND SUPPLICATION IN THE SPIRIT, BEING WATCHFUL TO THIS END WITH ALL PERSEVERANCE AND SUPPLICATION FOR ALL THE SAINTS.
EPHESIANS 6:10-18

There are many enlisted, yet so few engaged.

THE CROSS

> **To live free is to recognize that your flesh has been crucified with Christ, and the life you live today is free from sin and death. It is to recognize that your flesh has been crucified with Christ. It was on the cross that Jesus sacrificed His life in your place to atone for the sins of all humanity. The cross of Christ was both God's justice for sin and mercy for sinners.**

As a believer, it's important to know that Jesus accomplished several things related to His death on the cross. Jesus' death satisfied the curse upon mankind and cleansed us from our sin nature (1 John 3:5). It took care of the penalty for our sin and the wrath of the Father (John 3:36). His death destroyed the works of the devil (1 John 3:8). Jesus suffered on the cross to bring us to God, being put to death in the flesh but made alive in the Spirit (1 Peter 3:18). Jesus took all of our sorrow, grief, and pain on the cross, and by His stripes we are healed (Isaiah 53). It was at the cross that Jesus atoned for our sin and brought us to God by His own blood.

FOR CHRIST ALSO SUFFERED ONCE FOR SINS, THE JUST FOR THE UNJUST, THAT HE MIGHT BRING US TO GOD, BEING PUT TO DEATH IN THE FLESH BUT MADE ALIVE BY THE SPIRIT. 1 PETER 3:18

AND YOU, BEING DEAD IN TRESPASSES AND THE UNCIRCUMCISION OF YOUR FLESH, HE HAS MADE ALIVE TOGETHER WITH HIM, HAVING FORGIVEN YOU ALL TRESPASSES, HAVING WIPED OUT THE HANDWRITING OF REQUIREMENTS THAT WAS AGAINST US, WHICH WAS CONTRARY TO US. AND HE HAS TAKEN IT OUT OF THE WAY, HAVING NAILED IT TO THE CROSS. HAVING DISARMED PRINCIPALITIES AND POWERS, HE MADE A PUBLIC SPECTACLE OF THEM, TRIUMPHING OVER THEM IN IT.
COLOSSIANS 2:13-15

HAVING ABOLISHED IN HIS FLESH THE ENMITY, THAT IS, THE LAW OF COMMANDMENTS CONTAINED IN ORDINANCES, SO AS TO CREATE IN HIMSELF ONE NEW MAN FROM THE TWO, THUS MAKING PEACE, AND THAT HE MIGHT RECONCILE THEM BOTH TO GOD IN ONE BODY THROUGH THE CROSS, THEREBY PUTTING TO DEATH THE ENMITY.
EPHESIANS 2:15-16

LIVING SANCTIFIED

To live free in Christ is to live a life that is separated from the world and set apart for holiness. We are called to worship the Lord in the beauty of His holiness. God has chosen to dwell among His people through His Holy Spirit. We are the temple of the Holy Spirit.

We are being conformed more and more into the image of Jesus Christ through the sanctifying power of the Holy Spirit.

Sanctification is important to the believer's life because it involves us being set apart unto God through holiness. Sanctification is the way God has set us apart for His glory. Sanctification can be viewed as three steps. The first step is positional. We were sanctified the moment we were saved. We now have the Holy Spirit living in us. The second step is practical. We daily are being sanctified through the working of the Holy Spirit and producing evidence or the fruit of the Holy Spirit within our lives. The third step is progressive. This is the sanctification work of the Holy Spirit in our lives that ultimately fulfills itself in eternity through glorification. The beauty is that we have been sanctified (past), we are being sanctified (present), and we will be sanctified (future) because God is working in us for His purpose and glory.

DO YOU NOT KNOW THAT YOU ARE THE TEMPLE OF GOD AND THAT THE SPIRIT OF GOD DWELLS IN YOU? IF ANYONE DEFILES THE TEMPLE OF GOD, GOD WILL DESTROY HIM. FOR THE TEMPLE OF GOD IS HOLY, WHICH TEMPLE YOU ARE.
1 CORINTHIANS 3:16-17

DO YOU KNOW THAT YOUR BODY IS THE TEMPLE OF THE HOLY SPIRIT WHO IS IN YOU, WHOM YOU HAVE FROM GOD, AND YOU ARE NOT YOUR OWN? FOR YOU WERE BOUGHT AT A PRICE; THEREFORE GLORIFY GOD IN YOUR BODY AND IN YOUR SPIRIT, WHICH ARE GOD'S.
1 CORINTHIANS 1:6:19-20

DO YOU NOT KNOW THAT THE UNRIGHTEOUS WILL NOT INHERIT THE KINGDOM OF GOD? DO NOT BE DECEIVED. NEITHER FORNICATORS, NOR IDOLATERS, NOR ADULTERERS, NOR HOMOSEXUALS, NOR SODOMITES, NOR THIEVES, NOR COVETOUS, NOR DRUNKARDS, NOR REVILERS, NOR EXTORTIONERS WILL INHERIT THE KINGDOM OF GOD. AND SUCH WERE SOME OF YOU. BUT YOU WERE WASHED, BUT YOU WERE SANCTIFIED, BUT YOU WERE JUSTIFIED IN THE NAME OF THE LORD JESUS AND BY THE SPIRIT OF OUR GOD.
1 CORINTHIANS 6:9-11

FOR YOU KNOW WHAT COMMANDMENTS WE GAVE YOU THROUGH THE LORD JESUS. FOR THIS IS THE WILL OF GOD, YOUR SANCTIFICATION: THAT YOU SHOULD ABSTAIN FROM SEXUAL IMMORALITY ...

... THAT EACH OF YOU SHOULD KNOW HOW TO POSSESS HIS OWN VESSEL IN SANCTIFICATION AND HONOR.
1 THESSALONIANS 4:2-4

NOW MAY THE GOD OF PEACE HIMSELF SANCTIFY YOU COMPLETELY; AND MAY YOUR WHOLE SPIRIT, SOUL, AND BODY BE PRESERVED BLAMELESS AT THE COMING OF OUR LORD JESUS CHRIST.
1 THESSALONIANS 5:23

DISCOVER ///
Truth/Scripture Insight/Spirit Insight

Read Ephesians 2:1-5.
Who and what <u>were</u> you before coming to Jesus Christ?

_____

Who and what <u>are</u> you after coming to Jesus Christ?

_____

What have you been saved by?

_____

Read Luke 4:1-11 and 1 John 2:15-17.
Where do temptations come from?

_____

How do we overcome temptations?

_____

Read James 4:7.
When engaged in spiritual warfare, what should we do first?

_____

Read Ephesians 6:10-18.
What is the real source of many of our struggles?

_____

What are the different parts of the armor of God?

_____

_____

Read Colossians 2:13-14.
What did God do through the cross?

_____

_____

Sanctification
In your own words, what does sanctification mean?

_____

_____

DECIDE ///
Change of Mind/Believe

What areas of temptation do you find most difficult to overcome? _____

_____

What specific actions do you need to take in order to strengthen areas of weakness (information, activities, accountability)? _____

_____

_____

DO ///
Commit/Take Action

How will you commit to living free?

_____

What specific actions do you need to take in order to strengthen areas of weakness (information, activities, accountability)? _____

_____

_____

_____

_____

DEVOTE ///
Invest Time/Continue

What will you invest your time in this week that will help you stay away from temptation and sin? _____

_____

_____

_____

_____

DEVELOP ///
Experience/Abide

List three ways you can better experience Christ this week:

1. _____
2. _____
3. _____

MEMORIZE ///

AND YOU SHALL KNOW THE TRUTH, AND
THE TRUTH SHALL MAKE YOU FREE. ...
THEREFORE IF THE SON MAKES YOU FREE,
YOU SHALL BE FREE INDEED.
JOHN 8:32, 36

IF WE CONFESS
OUR SINS, HE IS
FAITHFUL AND
JUST TO FORGIVE
US OUR SINS
AND TO CLEANSE
US FROM ALL
UNRIGHTEOUSNESS.
1 JOHN 1:9

LIVE LIFE :: LIVE FORGIVEN

TOPICS COVERED

RELATIONSHIPS – GOD/OTHERS

CONFESSION AND FORGIVENESS

RECEIVING GOD'S GRACE

LIVING RECONCILED

LIVE LIFE :::
LIVE FORGIVEN

RELATIONSHIPS – GOD/OTHERS

> We live in a fallen world where people and things are not functioning the way God has intended. This world is truly broken. Life is hard. We daily face all kinds of challenges and difficulties, and it feels like nothing ever goes our way. As a result, most of our relationships fail because they never seem to match our expectations and end in disaster. Too often the lack of forgiveness is replaced with anger and bitterness.
>
> Let's face it—everyone has relationship issues. The greatest relationship problem we have is with God. So how do we fix it?

Let's begin with our relationship with God. We are separated from God before coming to Jesus. How amazing it is when we discover that the Gospel is the glue that puts us back together. Only God can fix our relationship issues. If our relationship with God is right, then our relationship with others will realign. When we readjust and align our relationships with how God designed them, then we will see the importance of loving God and loving others. Our relationships with others depend on our relationship with God, which begins when we receive His love and forgiveness.

WE LOVE HIM BECAUSE HE FIRST LOVED US. 1 JOHN 4:19

IF GOD SO LOVED US, WE ALSO OUGHT TO LOVE ONE ANOTHER. 1 JOHN 4:11

Jesus summarized all of the Law into two great commandments. In doing so, the consistent theme that we discover is love. Love God and love others. True love involves the heart, the soul, the mind, and all of our strength. To live life forgiven is to receive God's love and properly respond by loving Him back. As a believer, when we experience God's love, it is so strong that it motivates us to properly love others.

"YOU SHALL LOVE THE LORD YOUR GOD WITH ALL YOUR HEART, WITH ALL YOUR SOUL, AND WITH ALL YOUR MIND." THIS ...

> **... IS THE FIRST AND GREAT COMMANDMENT. AND THE SECOND IS LIKE IT: "YOU SHALL LOVE YOUR NEIGHBOR AS YOURSELF." ON THESE TWO COMMANDMENTS HANG ALL THE LAW AND THE PROPHETS.**
> MATTHEW 22:37-40

Notice that these two commands fulfill the biblical requirements known as the Law and the Prophets. They also portray a picture of the cross for us. When our vertical relationship with God is right, then our horizontal relationships with others will be right as well. Most people come to Christ because of a relationship. Some come to Christ because someone in their life cared enough about them to bring them to church or an event to hear the Gospel. Some come to Christ because they recently went through a divorce or breakup. Some come to Christ because of a recent tragedy. Others just received news that they have cancer and that they have a short time to live. Regardless of the reason, it all comes back to relationship. We remain separated in our relationship with God until we receive Christ as our Savior. Once we reconnect with Him, then we can reconnect our relationships with others.

To live life forgiven is to receive God's love and properly respond by loving Him back.

BUT GOD DEMONSTRATES HIS OWN LOVE TOWARD US, IN THAT WHILE WE WERE STILL SINNERS, CHRIST DIED FOR US. MUCH MORE THEN, HAVING NOW BEEN JUSTIFIED BY HIS BLOOD, WE SHALL BE SAVED FROM WRATH THROUGH HIM.
ROMANS 5:8-9

God has proved His love for us by Christ's death on the cross.

AS FAR AS THE EAST IS FROM THE WEST, SO FAR HAS HE REMOVED OUR TRANSGRESSIONS FROM US.
PSALM 103:12

FOR HE MADE HIM WHO KNEW NO SIN TO BE SIN FOR US, THAT WE MIGHT BECOME THE RIGHTEOUSNESS OF GOD IN HIM.
2 CORINTHIANS 5:21

CONFESSION AND FORGIVENESS

IF MY PEOPLE WHO ARE CALLED BY MY NAME WILL HUMBLE THEMSELVES, AND PRAY AND SEEK MY FACE, AND TURN FROM THEIR WICKED WAYS, THEN I WILL HEAR FROM HEAVEN, AND WILL FORGIVE THEIR SIN AND HEAL THEIR LAND.
2 CHRONICLES 7:14

LOOK ON MY AFFLICTION AND MY PAIN, AND FORGIVE ALL MY SINS.
PSALM 25:18

FOR YOU, LORD, ARE GOOD, AND READY TO FORGIVE, AND ABUNDANT IN MERCY TO ALL THOSE WHO CALL UPON YOU.
PSALM 86:5

In these Scriptures, a pattern takes shape regarding forgiveness that is important for us to recognize and apply to our lives. To live forgiven is to humbly pray and confess all known sins to God, turn from those sins, and turn back to God. Are you actively calling upon God to forgive and cleanse you from sin?

Once a believer receives the love of God and asks for forgiveness, the results are healing, restoration, renewal, and life. Without forgiveness, people remain imprisoned in their own denial, bitterness, anger, rage, despair, and disappointment. To live life forgiven is to experience true freedom from guilt, shame, self-condemnation, and bitterness.

"COME NOW, AND LET US REASON TOGETHER," SAYS THE LORD. "THOUGH YOUR SINS ARE LIKE SCARLET, THEY WILL BE WHITE AS SNOW; THOUGH THEY ARE RED LIKE CRIMSON, THEY WILL BE AS WOOL." ISAIAH 1:18

God invites us to "reason" with Him. He doesn't say, let's reason in a few weeks or a few days, but rather He emphasizes the present. Right now, today! God wants to deal with our sin today and wash it away because it has stained our souls. Our sins are like scarlet and crimson red, and only He can wash out the stain of sin to make us white as snow and clean as wool. Forgiveness is available today. Let us be reasonable and receive His offer.

Are you willing to reason together with God? Are you willing to surrender your guilty conscience and allow Him to take away the despair and shame of your sin and accept His forgiveness?

Why are so many people bitter and unwilling to forgive? The simple answer is that, for the unbeliever, they haven't yet experienced the power of God's forgiveness in their own life. Most relationships without God are shallow. It's difficult to have meaningful relationships without God simply because they are often very one-sided. A person who is bitter or unforgiving can only see their side of the relationship, and because of pride, they remain one-sided. Until they believe and receive Christ, they often remain in a place of selfishness, pride, and bitterness. They struggle and fight to hold on to what they feel is right, yet eventually every relationship they do have slowly decays or simply falls apart. Unless you experience a right relationship with God first, all other relationships will seem meaningless. Literally, kingdoms have been divided due to bad relationships. Divorce is all too common. History shows us over and over again that without reconciliation and true forgiveness, bitterness will always get the upper hand every time. There are way too many people who are divided, lonely, and broken because an apology was never spoken. What about you? Is there someone that you need to forgive? Are you living a bitter life? Are you truly living life forgiven and forgiving others?

FORGIVING OTHERS

> **"You will cast all our sins into the depths of the sea" (Micah 7:19).**

> To live forgiven is to be a receiver of God's grace and a distributor of His mercy to others. Learning to forgive others is replicating the nature of Jesus.

THIS IS MY COMMANDMENT, THAT YOU LOVE ONE ANOTHER AS I HAVE LOVED YOU. GREATER LOVE HAS NO ONE THAN THIS, THAN TO LAY DOWN ONE'S LIFE FOR HIS FRIENDS. JOHN 15:12-13

IF SOMEONE SAYS, "I LOVE GOD," AND HATES HIS BROTHER, HE IS A LIAR; FOR HE WHO DOES NOT LOVE HIS BROTHER WHOM HE HAS SEEN, HOW CAN HE LOVE GOD WHOM HE HAS NOT SEEN? AND THIS COMMANDMENT WE HAVE FROM HIM: THAT HE WHO LOVES GOD MUST LOVE HIS BROTHER ALSO. 1 JOHN 4:20-21

How important do you think it is to forgive others for the wrongs they have done? Let's see what Jesus says about it.

> **FOR IF YOU FORGIVE MEN THEIR TRESPASSES, YOUR HEAVENLY FATHER WILL ALSO FORGIVE YOU. BUT IF YOU DO NOT FORGIVE MEN THEIR TRESPASSES, NEITHER WILL YOUR FATHER FORGIVE YOUR TRESPASSES.** MATTHEW 6:14-15

These happen to be some of the strongest words that Jesus spoke related to the importance of forgiving others. It's critical that we trust God by letting go of the past and truly forgive others who have sinned against us because it affects our relationship with God. **To live life forgiven involves forgiving those who have purposely sinned against us.** It's not easy to forgive those who have hurt, abused, or abandoned us, but remember, if God tells us to do it, He also will give us the power to do it. God knows that what we hold on to from the past will keep us from experiencing His power in the present. As we let go and truly ask God to help us forgive, we will see God do great and mighty things!

How are we to deal with personal conflict and find a resolution?

> **THEREFORE IF YOU BRING YOUR GIFT TO THE ALTAR, AND THERE REMEMBER THAT YOUR BROTHER HAS SOMETHING ...**

... AGAINST YOU, LEAVE YOUR GIFT THERE BEFORE THE ALTAR, AND GO YOUR WAY. FIRST BE RECONCILED TO YOUR BROTHER, AND THEN COME AND OFFER YOUR GIFT.
MATTHEW 5:23-24

When there is conflict in a relationship, we are told in Scripture what steps we are to take to make things right. The principle is that before we worship God by offering our tithes or our resources, we need to be at peace and in right relationships with others. It is more important to God that our consciences are free and that nothing interferes or distracts us from worshiping God. The key is to be reconciled with one another. In life we will experience conflict. It can't be avoided. However, when conflict arises, even if we are in the right and the other person is holding on to a grudge, we must do all we can to bring resolution. Resolution seeks to find the answer to the wrong. **Reconciliation seeks to restore unity and peace within a divided relationship.**

Recognize that some differences may never be resolved, but we can still submit ourselves to God and commit these differences to Him in prayer, asking for a resolution. It's never easy when we find ourselves wanting to make things right in a divided relationship but the other person doesn't want to. The issue here is for us to get our hearts right with God first, regardless of the outcome. God wants us to be reconciled to Him and others. God wants us to be at peace with everyone.

> FOR HE WHO SERVES CHRIST IN THESE THINGS IS ACCEPTABLE TO GOD AND APPROVED BY MEN. THEREFORE LET US PURSUE THE THINGS WHICH MAKE FOR PEACE AND THE THINGS BY WHICH ONE MAY EDIFY ANOTHER. ROMANS 14:18-19

RECEIVING GOD'S GRACE

To live life forgiven is to come with a surrendered heart and open hand, freely receiving God's grace. Grace transforms our lives.

It is so easy to be discontent. We get irritated and impatient with ourselves and those around us. We often complain and are dissatisfied. Whenever we put ourselves first in the center of our world and not God, we find plenty of things to complain about. We try to meet unrealistic expectations, and we fail. We find ourselves stressed out, anxious, and doubting, wondering if God has forgotten about us and if He really loves us. We are not alone; we all go through these types of feelings, and God knows that we do. This is why it's important to know that God's grace never fails us. God's grace never changes. His mercies are new every morning, and we can rest in and rely upon them.

Jeremiah, an Old Testament prophet, reminds us of how God's grace changes our outlook in times of distress and despair.

> I CALLED ON YOUR NAME, O LORD, FROM THE LOWEST PIT. YOU HAVE HEARD MY VOICE: "DO NOT HIDE YOUR EAR FROM MY SIGHING, FROM MY CRY FOR HELP." YOU DREW NEAR ON THE DAY I CALLED ON YOU, AND SAID TO ME, "DO NOT FEAR!" O LORD, YOU HAVE PLEADED THE CASE FOR MY SOUL; YOU HAVE REDEEMED MY LIFE. LAMENTATIONS 3:55-58

> THROUGH THE LORD'S MERCIES WE ARE NOT CONSUMED, BECAUSE HIS COMPASSIONS FAIL NOT. THEY ARE NEW EVERY MORNING; GREAT IS YOUR FAITHFULNESS. LAMENTATIONS 3:22-23

Unfortunately, many people still live with their failures and are stuck in the moment, not fully believing in His grace and forgiveness. They feel it is wrong to accept God's grace, especially if they are still hurting and grieving over their sins. It is God's desire that we accept His grace and forgiveness and take the next step to healing.

FOR BY GRACE YOU HAVE BEEN SAVED THROUGH FAITH, AND THAT NOT OF YOURSELVES; IT IS THE GIFT OF GOD, NOT OF WORKS, LEST ANYONE SHOULD BOAST. EPHESIANS 2:8-9

FOR THE GRACE OF GOD THAT BRINGS SALVATION HAS APPEARED TO ALL MEN. TITUS 2:11

LET US THEREFORE COME BOLDLY TO THE THRONE OF GRACE, THAT WE MAY OBTAIN MERCY AND FIND GRACE TO HELP IN TIME OF NEED. HEBREWS 4:16

LIVING RECONCILED

Reconciliation means to bring together that which was separated at war. Reconciliation is not a temporary truce; it is a permanent solution that God accomplished by reconciling us to Himself. Sinners need to be reconciled to God. Reconciliation allows us to be ambassadors for Christ.

NOW ALL THINGS ARE OF GOD, WHO HAS RECONCILED US TO HIMSELF THROUGH JESUS CHRIST, AND HAS GIVEN US THE MINISTRY OF RECONCILIATION, THAT IS, THAT GOD WAS IN CHRIST RECONCILING THE WORLD TO HIMSELF, NOT IMPUTING THEIR TRESPASSES TO THEM, AND HAS COMMITTED TO US THE WORD OF RECONCILIATION. NOW THEN, WE ARE AMBASSADORS FOR CHRIST, AS THOUGH GOD WERE PLEADING THROUGH US: WE IMPLORE YOU ON CHRIST'S BEHALF, BE RECONCILED TO GOD.
2 CORINTHIANS 5:18-20

To better understand reconciliation, let's consider the Roman Empire. Rome had two kinds of provinces: senatorial and imperial. These two provinces were vastly different. The senatorial provinces were ruled well, and the people lived in peace, needing little to no military occupation. The imperial provinces were restless and warlike and needed military support often. The emperor ruled the imperial provinces directly through his troops and always sent ambassadors to those provinces to bring peace. The fact that God has called us to be His ambassadors in this world is an indication our world is an imperial province at war with God and in need of being reconciled to God. To live life forgiven involves being reconciled to God because when we were enemies, we were reconciled to Him through the death of His Son.

To live life forgiven involves being reconciled to God.

> FOR IF WHEN WE WERE ENEMIES WE WERE RECONCILED TO GOD THROUGH THE DEATH OF HIS SON, MUCH MORE, HAVING BEEN RECONCILED, WE SHALL BE SAVED BY HIS LIFE. AND NOT ONLY THAT, BUT WE ALSO REJOICE IN GOD THROUGH OUR LORD JESUS CHRIST, THROUGH WHOM WE HAVE NOW RECEIVED THE RECONCILIATION. ROMANS 5:10-11

The Scriptures tell us that friendship with the world is enmity with God. Mankind is separated from God and needs to be brought back into a right relationship with Him. Mankind lives for the world and the flesh, and his motive is self-glory, interested only in pleasing himself. However, Jesus loves and reconciles the lost sinner.

It was Adam who ran and hid from God, and after Adam sinned, God went and sought him out. God called to Adam, "Where are you?" God never forsook man. It was Adam who was felt guilty and shameful. Sin always brings guilt and shame. But God called out to him and rescued him. This is why God sent His Son to rescue us. The more you love someone, the more you hate and despise the bad things they do. God removes all the obstacles that stand between us. Reconciliation eliminates the obstacles and permanently brings us back together for God's glory.

FOR IT PLEASED THE FATHER THAT IN HIM ALL THE FULLNESS SHOULD DWELL, AND BY HIM TO RECONCILE ALL THINGS TO HIMSELF, BY HIM, WHETHER THINGS ON EARTH OR THINGS IN HEAVEN, HAVING MADE PEACE THROUGH THE BLOOD OF HIS CROSS. AND YOU, WHO ONCE WERE ALIENATED AND ENEMIES IN YOUR MIND BY WICKED WORKS, YET NOW HE HAS ...

> **... RECONCILED IN THE BODY OF HIS FLESH THROUGH DEATH, TO PRESENT YOU HOLY, AND BLAMELESS, AND ABOVE REPROACH IN HIS SIGHT.** COLOSSIANS 1:19-22

DISCOVER ///
Truth/Scripture Insight/Spirit Insight

Read Matthew 22:34-40.
What are our two greatest loves supposed to be?

_____

How do we receive God's love?

_____

_____

Read 2 Corinthians 5:17-21.
How is our relationship with God fixed?

_____

What is that relationship based on?

_____

_____

Confession and Forgiveness

What is the result of confession and forgiveness?

_____

Why do people hold on to bitterness?

_____

What are a few things you are holding on to?

_____

Forgiving Others

To live forgiven is to be a receiver of God's:

_____

Why is it important that we let go of the past and forgive others?

_____

_____

Read 1 John 1:9.

When engaged in spiritual warfare, what should we do first?

_____

Read Ephesians 6:10-18.

What do we need to do when we sin?

_____

_____

What do you need to confess today?

_____

How often should we confess?

_____

DECIDE ///
Change of Mind/Believe

What negative things in my life (thoughts or actions) need to change? _____

_____

_____

What positive things (thoughts or actions) need to increase in my life? _____

_____

_____

DEVOTE ///
Invest Time/Continue

Write down one or two people that you need to forgive and be reconciled with. Begin to pray for them. Now, write a short letter, asking them to forgive you and let them know you've also forgiven them. Read the letters out loud to yourself when you finish, pray over it, asking God to give you strength to move forward. Now tear up the letter and throw it away. Next, begin to ask the Lord to provide the time for you to go in person and follow through with reconciliation. Healing happens when you invest time to forgive.

DEVELOP ///
Experience/Abide

Daily practice:
Read 1 Corinthians 13:4-8 and review God's definition of love.

Every evening, review the day in light of this passage.

What specific thoughts or actions at home, work, school, and in your daily life did not match up to this passage?

What could have been done differently?

_____

_____

_____

_____

MEMORIZE ///

IF WE CONFESS OUR SINS, HE IS FAITHFUL AND JUST TO FORGIVE US OUR SINS AND TO CLEANSE US FROM ALL UNRIGHTEOUSNESS. 1 JOHN 1:9

I AM THE RESURRECTION AND THE LIFE. HE WHO BELIEVES IN ME, THOUGH HE MAY DIE, HE SHALL LIVE. AND WHOEVER LIVES AND BELIEVES IN ME SHALL NEVER DIE. DO YOU BELIEVE THIS?

JOHN 11:25-26

LIVE LIFE :.: LIVE FOREVER

TOPICS COVERED

THE POWER OF A RESURRECTED LIFE

THE HOLY SPIRIT

HEAVEN

THE FUTURE

LIVING GLORIFIED

LIVE LIFE :::
LIVE FOREVER

THE POWER OF A RESURRECTED LIFE

To live forever with God is what every believer is looking forward to and preparing for. Eternal life is more than the quantity of life, it's the quality of life that God has promised. We invest our time, talent, and treasure for an eternal reward. The reward we look forward to and will receive is an actual place called Heaven—the very place and presence of God. What if it was possible to experience eternal life and a taste of Heaven today?

Did you know that how we define life determines our destiny? Did you know that our perspective influences our daily decisions? How we invest our time, spend our money, and develop our relationships are connected to what we value most in life. For many, life is all about survival. They live life, simply working to make ends meet. They live week by week hoping that someday they might get a break, pulling themselves up by their bootstraps. They are **survivalists**. Next, there are those who live by the roll of the dice or by the cards they have been dealt. They live life by chance or the luck of the draw. In addition, they play the lottery, hoping to hit it big and go out with a bang. They are **gamblers**.

And what about those who live life as a race? They view life as a competition, racing through everything in a hurry. Their end goal is to finish the race in first place. They will do anything to win, even if it means compromising their values and forfeiting friendships. They are **competitors**. And finally, there are those who view life as a marathon. They have moral standards and their intentions are good. They value endurance. They pace themselves throughout life; they plan for safe retirement and dream of resting someday. They are consistently investing in their earthly comfort. They are **self-sufficient survivors**. However, they completely miss out on a greater and more valuable investment that pays off in the end—**Heaven!**

How do you define your life? How are you living your life today? What do you value most? Where do you spend most of your time?

DO NOT LAY UP FOR YOURSELVES TREASURES ON EARTH, WHERE MOTH AND RUST DESTROY AND WHERE THIEVES BREAK IN AND STEAL; BUT LAY UP FOR YOURSELVES TREASURES IN HEAVEN, WHERE NEITHER MOTH NOR RUST DESTROYS AND WHERE THIEVES DO NOT BREAK IN AND STEAL.
ISAIAH 1:18

> **FOR WHERE YOUR TREASURE IS, THERE YOUR HEART WILL BE ALSO.**
> MATTHEW 6:21

The power of the resurrected life is essential for the believer. Two statements summarize this power. Jesus spoke of it in John 15:5, "for without Me you can do nothing." And Paul said in Philippians 4:13, "I can do all things through Christ who strengthens me." To live life in the power of the Spirit is to know that I can do all things through Christ, but without Christ I can do nothing. It seems simple, but so often we find ourselves lacking the power to live life for Christ because we are overcome by temptation and sin. It's usually after we fail that we realize we tried to do something outside of God's will. We failed because we attempted to do something without Christ's approval. Remember, without Christ, we can nothing, but with Christ, we can do all things. Read the set of Scriptures that promise the evidence of the Holy Spirit working in us to accomplish His will and His work.

> **FOR IT IS GOD WHO WORKS IN YOU BOTH TO WILL AND TO DO FOR HIS GOOD PLEASURE.** PHILIPPIANS 2:13

BEING CONFIDENT OF THIS VERY THING, THAT HE WHO HAS BEGUN A GOOD WORK IN YOU WILL COMPLETE IT UNTIL THE DAY OF JESUS CHRIST. PHILIPPIANS 1:6

BEHOLD WHAT MANNER OF LOVE THE FATHER HAS BESTOWED ON US, THAT WE SHOULD BE CALLED CHILDREN OF GOD! THEREFORE, THE WORLD DOES NOT KNOW US, BECAUSE IT DID NOT KNOW HIM. BELOVED, NOW WE ARE CHILDREN OF GOD; AND IT HAS NOT YET BEEN REVEALED WHAT WE SHALL BE, BUT WE KNOW THAT WHEN HE IS REVEALED, WE SHALL BE LIKE HIM, FOR WE SHALL SEE HIM AS HE IS. AND EVERYONE WHO HAS THIS HOPE IN HIM PURIFIES HIMSELF, JUST AS HE IS PURE. 1 JOHN 3:1-4

To live life forever is to believe that God lives in us. He who began this new work in us is faithful to complete it. God has given us all that we need to live the resurrected life. The resurrected life is a life that has overcome sin and death.

NOW MAY THE GOD OF PEACE WHO BROUGHT UP OUR LORD JESUS FROM THE DEAD, THAT GREAT SHEPHERD OF THE SHEEP, THROUGH THE BLOOD OF THE EVERLASTING COVENANT, MAKE YOU COMPLETE IN EVERY GOOD WORK TO DO HIS WILL, WORKING IN YOU WHAT IS WELL PLEASING IN HIS SIGHT, THROUGH JESUS CHRIST, TO WHOM BE GLORY FOREVER AND EVER. AMEN. HEBREWS 13:20-21

God has given us all we need to live the resurrected life. To live forever is to acknowledge the Person and Presence of the Holy Spirit within our lives. We are the temple of the Holy Spirit, and the Spirit gives us life. The Holy Spirit dwells within us and allows us to experience the quality of eternal life in the present.

What happened when you accepted, believed, and confessed Jesus as your Lord? What took place the moment you turned

from your sin and received Jesus as your personal Savior? The simple answer is that the Holy Spirit came into your life and began a new work. We need to realize that God loves us so much, and He who began this new work in our lives is faithful to complete it.

> **BUT IF THE SPIRIT OF HIM WHO RAISED JESUS FROM THE DEAD DWELLS IN YOU, HE WHO RAISED CHRIST FROM THE DEAD WILL ALSO GIVE LIFE TO YOUR MORTAL BODIES THROUGH HIS SPIRIT WHO DWELLS IN YOU.** ROMANS 8:11

The Holy Spirit is daily conforming us into the image of Christ. He accomplishes this by working in us, refining us, and redefining us to be like Him. We express the presence of God in our lives by visible evidence. **How do we see the evidence of the Holy Spirit in our lives?**

THE HOLY SPIRIT

> **The Holy Spirit is the Helper who teaches and leads us into all truth. The Father sent the Holy Spirit in Jesus' name to dwell with us, to be in us, and most importantly, to be upon us. We experience His**

presence most when He takes permanent residence in us. He brings comfort and peace to the believer. The essential role of the Holy Spirit is to convict the world of sin, righteousness, and judgment by drawing all people to a loving relationship with Jesus.

The Holy Spirit is known as the third person of the Trinity. In Romans 8, we are told that the Holy Spirit raised Jesus from the dead and that He now dwells in the believer. It's important to realize that the Holy Spirit gives us true life. It's one thing to believe that someday, in our "immortal bodies," we will experience eternal life; it's quite another thing to actually experience eternal life in our "mortal bodies" today.

To live forever starts by daily relying upon the power of the Holy Spirit.

There are several examples in Scripture that define the Holy Spirit as being the third person of the Trinity. He is described as the Spirit of Christ, the Spirit of Truth, the Spirit of Grace, and the Eternal Spirit. The Holy Spirit is God. One example in Scripture that equates the Holy Spirit with the Godhead is in Matthew 28:19, "Go therefore and make disciples of all nations, baptizing them in the name of the Father and of the Son and the Holy Spirit." Notice that Matthew uses the word "the" to properly distinguish the Godhead Trinity of the Father, the Son, and the Holy Spirit. It's important for us to understand that when we pray, we pray in the Holy Spirit, through Jesus Christ, and to the Father. The Holy Spirit's role is vital to the Christian life.

The Holy Spirit works in three primary ways in the life of the believer. He promises to be with the believer, dwell in the believer, and pour out His power upon the believer.

The Holy Spirit is "with" all people (convicting the world of sin, righteousness, and judgment), **"in"** (received at time of personal salvation), and **"upon"** (experienced at time of baptism with the Spirit).

With (*para*) "And I will pray the Father, and He will give you another Helper, that He may abide **with you forever**—the Spirit of truth, whom the world cannot receive, because it neither sees Him nor knows Him; but you know Him, for **He dwells with you and will be in you**" (John 14:16-17).

In (*en*) After Jesus' resurrection, He appeared to His disciples, "And when He had said this, **He breathed on them**, and said to them, '**Receive the Holy Spirit**'" (John 20:22).

Upon (*epi*) "But you shall receive **power** when the **Holy Spirit** has come **upon** you; and you shall be **witnesses to Me** in Jerusalem, and in all Judea and Samaria, and to the end of the earth" (Acts 1:8).

DIG DEEPER: Research how the Holy Spirit empowers believers with gifts, ministries, and ways to serve as members of Christ's body on earth (Romans 12:3-8 / Ephesians 4:7-16). Learn how He equips believers with the tools to carry out their calling with effectiveness (1 Corinthians 12:1-31).

HEAVEN

Every civilization has been shaped by the belief that Heaven is a real place, and we are destined to go there after death. However, there is only one true God and one true Heaven. Jesus made a way for us to become permanent residents in Heaven. It is the ultimate destination for those who follow Jesus Christ. Heaven is more than a destination; it's a motivation. If we live our life believing that every action on earth would have eternal impact and reward, how different would we live life today?

To live forever begins by knowing that Heaven is a real place and that my life has meaning and purpose today. Heaven is God's dwelling place. We will live life with Him, and we will experience no more pain, sorrow, or death. Old things that brought sorrow and pain will pass away and all things will be made new. To live forever is to experience the presence of God today.

NOW I SAW A NEW HEAVEN AND A NEW EARTH, FOR THE FIRST HEAVEN AND THE FIRST EARTH HAD PASSED AWAY. ALSO, THERE WAS NO MORE SEA. THEN I, JOHN, SAW THE HOLY CITY, NEW JERUSALEM, COMING DOWN OUT OF HEAVEN FROM GOD, PREPARED AS A BRIDE ADORNED ...

... FOR HER HUSBAND. AND I HEARD A LOUD VOICE FROM HEAVEN SAYING, "BEHOLD, THE TABERNACLE OF GOD IS WITH MEN, AND HE WILL DWELL WITH THEM, AND THEY SHALL BE HIS PEOPLE. GOD HIMSELF WILL BE WITH THEM AND BE THEIR GOD. AND GOD WILL WIPE AWAY EVERY TEAR FROM THEIR EYES; THERE SHALL BE NO MORE DEATH, NOR SORROW, NOR CRYING. THERE SHALL BE NO MORE PAIN, FOR THE FORMER THINGS HAVE PASSED AWAY." REVELATION 21:1-4

It's important to know that no one goes to Heaven automatically. Jesus said to enter by the narrow gate, for wide is the gate and broad is the road that leads to destruction, and many enter through it. What keeps us out of Heaven is sin. Hell will be inhabited by those who have never received God's loving gift of redemption from Jesus Christ. How long will Hell last? Hell will be everlasting, according to Jesus. He said, "And these will go away into everlasting punishment, but the righteous into eternal life" (Matthew 25:46). There are only two possible destinations after death: Heaven and Hell. Both destinations are just as real and eternal as the other. From birth, we have all been set on autopilot toward Hell. We need to alter our direction, readjust, change lanes, and set our course for Heaven. Jesus is the way, the truth, and the life. To live forever is to travel on the right path.

To live forever means being assured that we are going to Heaven.

AND HE SHOWED ME A PURE RIVER OF WATER OF LIFE, CLEAR AS CRYSTAL, PROCEEDING FROM THE THRONE OF GOD AND OF THE LAMB. IN THE MIDDLE OF ITS STREET, AND ON EITHER SIDE OF THE RIVER, WAS THE TREE OF LIFE, WHICH BORE TWELVE FRUITS, EACH TREE YIELDING ITS FRUIT EVERY MONTH. THE LEAVES OF THE TREE WERE FOR THE HEALING OF THE NATIONS. AND THERE SHALL BE NO MORE CURSE, BUT THE THRONE OF GOD AND OF THE LAMB SHALL BE IN IT, AND HIS SERVANTS SHALL SERVE HIM. THEY SHALL SEE HIS FACE, AND HIS NAME SHALL BE ON THEIR FOREHEADS. THERE SHALL BE NO NIGHT THERE: THEY NEED NO LAMP NOR LIGHT OF THE SUN, FOR THE LORD GOD GIVES THEM LIGHT. AND THEY SHALL REIGN FOREVER AND EVER. REVELATION 22:1-5

THE FUTURE

To consider the future, we must consider mortality. The current death rate is 100 out of 100 people die. It is statistically known that three people die every second, 180 every minute, and nearly 11,000 every hour. That means that more than 250,000 people go to Heaven or Hell every day. If this is the current mortality rate, then we really need to consider our future destiny.

How and where will you spend eternity?

I love that Jesus spoke of Heaven often. Before Jesus went to the cross, He not only spoke about Heaven, He also encouraged His disciples not worry about their future. He had it all worked out. Jesus has a way of reminding His followers that living life for God will always be worth it. Heaven is a place worth living for today. **Jesus encouraged His disciples with these words about Heaven.**

LET NOT YOUR HEART BE TROUBLED; YOU BELIEVE IN GOD, BELIEVE ALSO IN ME. IN MY FATHER'S HOUSE ARE MANY MANSIONS; IF IT WERE NOT SO, I WOULD HAVE TOLD YOU. I GO TO PREPARE A PLACE FOR YOU. AND IF I GO AND PREPARE A PLACE FOR YOU, I WILL ...

... AGAIN AND RECEIVE YOU TO MYSELF; THAT WHERE I AM, THERE YOU MAY BE ALSO. JOHN 14:1-3

To live forever recognizes that Jesus is the way, the truth, and the life.

THAT WHICH WE HAVE SEEN AND HEARD WE DECLARE TO YOU, THAT YOU ALSO MAY HAVE FELLOWSHIP WITH US; AND TRULY OUR FELLOWSHIP IS WITH THE FATHER AND WITH HIS SON JESUS CHRIST. AND THESE THINGS WE WRITE TO YOU THAT YOUR JOY MAY BE FULL. 1 JOHN 1:3-4

AND YOU HE MADE ALIVE, WHO WERE DEAD IN TRESPASSES AND SINS, IN WHICH YOU ONCE WALKED ACCORDING TO THE COURSE OF THIS WORLD, ACCORDING TO THE PRINCE OF THE POWER OF THE AIR, THE SPIRIT WHO NOW WORKS IN THE SONS OF DISOBEDIENCE, AMONG WHOM ALSO WE ALL ONCE CONDUCTED OURSELVES IN THE LUSTS OF OUR FLESH, FULFILLING THE DESIRES OF THE FLESH AND OF THE MIND, AND WERE BY NATURE CHILDREN OF WRATH, JUST AS THE OTHERS. BUT GOD, WHO IS RICH IN MERCY, BECAUSE OF HIS GREAT LOVE WITH WHICH HE LOVED US, EVEN WHEN WE WERE DEAD IN TRESPASSES, MADE US ALIVE TOGETHER WITH CHRIST.
EPHESIANS 2:1-5

LIVING GLORIFIED

> **All that we do in the name of Jesus brings glory to God. Our desire is to walk worthy of the calling that God has for us. We have all fallen short of the glory of God. We were buried with Christ in baptism unto death. Just as Christ was raised from the dead by the glory of the Father, we should walk in the newness of life.**

Glorification occurs when believers receive their new bodies in the presence of the Lord. Ultimate glorification of the believer is to be completely sanctified into the image of Christ.

Whereas sanctification is the Christian's process of growth—being conformed to the image of Christ during this life—glorification is the believer's hope for the future in the presence of God. Think of living the glorified life as it relates to receiving your new celestial body. Living glorified is to inherit an incorruptible body. We are living for and looking forward to a spiritual body, like Christ. It will be raised in power and be immortal.

THE BODY IS SOWN IN CORRUPTION, IT IS RAISED IN INCORRUPTION. IT IS SOWN IN DISHONOR, IT IS RAISED IN GLORY. IT IS SOWN IN WEAKNESS, IT IS RAISED IN POWER. IT IS SOWN A NATURAL BODY, ...

... IT IS RAISED A SPIRITUAL BODY. THERE IS A NATURAL BODY, AND THERE IS A SPIRITUAL BODY. AND SO IT IS WRITTEN, 'THE FIRST MAN ADAM BECAME A LIVING BEING.' THE LAST ADAM BECAME A LIFE-GIVING SPIRIT. HOWEVER, THE SPIRITUAL IS NOT FIRST, BUT THE NATURAL, AND AFTERWARD THE SPIRITUAL. THE FIRST MAN WAS OF THE EARTH, MADE OF DUST; THE SECOND MAN IS THE LORD FROM HEAVEN. AS WAS THE MAN OF DUST, SO ALSO ARE THOSE WHO ARE MADE OF DUST; AND AS IS THE HEAVENLY MAN, SO ALSO ARE THOSE WHO ARE HEAVENLY. AND AS WE HAVE BORNE THE IMAGE OF THE MAN OF DUST, WE SHALL ALSO BEAR THE IMAGE OF THE HEAVENLY MAN. NOW THIS I SAY, BRETHREN, THAT FLESH AND BLOOD CANNOT INHERIT THE KINGDOM OF GOD; NOR DOES CORRUPTION INHERIT INCORRUPTION. BEHOLD, I TELL YOU A MYSTERY: WE SHALL NOT ALL SLEEP, BUT WE SHALL ALL BE CHANGED—IN ...

... A MOMENT, IN THE TWINKLING OF AN EYE, AT THE LAST TRUMPET. FOR THE TRUMPET WILL SOUND, AND THE DEAD WILL BE RAISED INCORRUPTIBLE, AND WE SHALL BE CHANGED. FOR THIS CORRUPTIBLE MUST PUT ON INCORRUPTION, AND THIS MORTAL MUST PUT ON IMMORTALITY. 1 CORINTHIANS 15:42-53

FOR THE LORD HIMSELF WILL DESCEND FROM HEAVEN WITH A SHOUT, WITH THE VOICE OF AN ARCHANGEL, AND WITH THE TRUMPET OF GOD. AND THE DEAD IN CHRIST WILL RISE FIRST. THEN WE WHO ARE ALIVE AND REMAIN SHALL BE CAUGHT UP TOGETHER WITH THEM IN THE CLOUDS TO MEET THE LORD IN THE AIR. AND THUS WE SHALL ALWAYS BE WITH THE LORD. 1 THESSALONIANS 4:16-17

DISCOVER ///
Truth/Scripture Insight/Spirit Insight

Read Philippians 3:19-21 and Matthew 6:19-21.
What are the two worlds the believer lives in?

_____

_____

Which one is eternal?

_____

_____

Which one is the best investment?

_____

_____

Read John 17:3.
How is eternal life defined?

_____

_____

_____

Read 2 Peter 3:9-12 and 1 John 3:2-3.
What difference does knowing you have eternal life (both a relationship and a location) make in your life today?

_____

_____

Read 2 Corinthians 4:17-18.
The direction of our life is often determined by what we focus our attention on. What does this verse mean in regard to our daily practice?

_____

_____

DECIDE ///
Change of Mind/Believe

In light of my current relationship with the Lord and my ultimate home with Him, what should my list of priorities look like?

_____

_____

Being faithful in the little things of life reveals character. What changes can be made so the little things achieve the big rewards? (Hint: attitude of serving the Lord)

_____

_____

DO ///
Commit/Take Action

Consider the following:
- What do my typical daily, weekly, and monthly schedules look like?
- What are my relationships (personal, work, school)?
- What tasks are on my to-do list?
- What do I waste time on?

What needs to be added so each thing becomes a service to God?

_____

_____

_____

_____

DEVOTE ///
Invest Time/Continue

How do I continue to walk in the power of the Holy Spirit?

_____

_____

_____

_____

DEVELOP ///
Experience/Abide

How am I practically exercising the gifts of the Holy Spirit in my daily life?

_____

_____

What are a few things I can adjust in my life to be more mindful of Heaven?

_____

_____

MEMORIZE ///

I AM THE RESURRECTION AND THE LIFE. HE WHO BELIEVES IN ME, THOUGH HE MAY DIE, HE SHALL LIVE. AND WHOEVER LIVES AND BELIEVES IN ME SHALL NEVER DIE. DO YOU BELIEVE THIS? JOHN 11:25-26

LIVE LIVE
DISCOVERING YOUR NEW LIFE IN CHRIST

Published by Calvary Publishing
3232 West MacArthur Boulevard
Santa Ana, CA 92704

First printing 2019

Cover layout and internal design and layout: Cory Emery

ISBN: 13:9-781597-511544

Printed in the United States of America.